ITALIAN
PICTURE DICTIONARY

© 2025 Rosetta Stone, LLC, a subsidiary of IXL Learning, Inc. All rights reserved. No part of this publication may be reproduced, stored in a retrieval system, or transmitted, in any form or by any means (electronic, mechanical, photocopying, recording, or otherwise) without the prior written permission of IXL Learning.

ISBN: 9781967345991

29 28 27 26 25 1 2 3 4 5

Printed in the USA

About this book

Are you ready to learn some Italian words? Before you begin, here's some useful information to help you get the most out of this book.

Il, lo, la, l', i, gli, and *le*

Most of the Italian words in this dictionary have **il, lo, la, l', i, gli,** or **le** in front of them. These words all mean *the*. So when you see **la mela**, it just means *the apple*. But why does Italian have so many different words for *the*?

You may already know that nouns can be *singular* or *plural*. Singular nouns refer to just one person, place, or thing, while plural nouns show more than one. In Italian, every noun is also either *masculine* or *feminine*. The word for *the* depends on whether a noun is singular, plural, masculine, or feminine—and what letters it starts with. Most masculine nouns use **il** when singular (e.g., **il gatto**) and **i** when plural (e.g., **i gatti**). Most feminine nouns use **la** when singular (e.g., **la mela**) and **le** when plural (e.g., **le mele**).

L' is used before any singular noun that starts with a vowel (a, e, i, o, u), like **l'acqua**. In this dictionary, words that use **l'** have an (m.) or (f.) next to them to show whether they are masculine or feminine.

There are also some singular nouns that use **lo** (e.g., **lo zucchero**) and some plural nouns that use **gli** (e.g. **gli orecchini**).

Italian symbols and letter pronunciation

Some words, like **caffè**, have little lines on top of them called *accents* that show which syllable carries *stress*. Pronounce a stressed syllable more forcefully than the other syllables in a word. For example, **caffè** is pronounced *kah-FEH*. If a word does not have an accent, the stress often falls on the second-to-last syllable of the word. For example, **delfino** is pronounced *dehl-FEE-noh*.

When you see the letter **c** before **e** or **i**, pronounce it like the *ch* in *cheese*. Before **a, o,** or **u**, pronounce it like the *c* in *cat*. So **noci** sounds like *NOH-chee*, while **cane** sounds like *KAH-neh*. But if there is an **s** before **ci** or **ce**, pronounce it like the *sh* in *sheep*. So **sciarpa** sounds like *SHAHR-pah*.

Similarly, a **g** before **e** or **i** sounds like the *j* in *judge*, but a **g** before **a, o,** or **u** sounds like the *g* in *go*. So **giacca** sounds like *JAH-kah*, while **aragosta** sounds like *ah-rah-GOH-stah*.

When **c** and **g** are followed by **he** or **hi**, pronounce them like *k* and *g*. So **cerchio** sounds like *CHEHR-kyoh*, and **traghetto** sounds like *trah-GEH-toh*.

The letter **z** can sound like *dz*, as in **zebra** (*DZEH-brah*), or like *ts*, as in **tazza** (*TAH-tsah*). And when you see **gn** in a word, pronounce it like *ny*. For example, **ragno** sounds like *RAH-nyoh*.

Saying words in Italian

The best way to learn how to say each word in Italian is to hear it spoken by a native Italian speaker. Scan the QR codes in this book to hear each word out loud. Under each Italian word in the dictionary, we also give you a guide on how to say the word.

Language facts

Throughout this book, we share fun, interesting, and useful facts about the Italian words you're learning.

Table of Contents

Numbers – I numeri 4
Colors – I colori 7
Shapes – Le forme 9
Animals – Gli animali 10
Fruits and vegetables – Frutta e verdura 19
Nuts – Le noci 28
Food – Il cibo 29
Drinks – Le bevande 35
Transportation – I mezzi di trasporto 36
Clothing and accessories – Abiti ed accessori 39
Shoes – Le scarpe 43
The body – Il corpo 44
Family – La famiglia 48
At home – A casa 50
In the kitchen – In cucina 55
At the table – A tavola 57
Bath time – Il bagno 59
At school – A scuola 61
Sports – Lo sport 63
Sports equipment – L'attrezzatura per lo sport 66
Useful phrases – Frasi utili 67
English-Italian A-Z 69

I numeri (Numbers)
ee NOO-meh-ree

0 zero
DZEH-roh
zero

1 uno
OO-noh
one

2 due
DOO-eh
two

3 tre
treh
three

4 quattro
KWAH-troh
four

5 cinque
CHEEN-kweh
five

6 sei
sey
six

7 sette
SEH-teh
seven

8 otto
OH-toh
eight

9 nove
NOH-veh
nine

10 dieci
DYEH-chee
ten

11 undici
OON-dee-chee
eleven

Scan here to hear the words!

12 dodici
DOH-dee-chee
twelve

13 tredici
TREH-dee-chee
thirteen

14 quattordici
kwah-TOR-dee-chee
fourteen

15 quindici
KWEEN-dee-chee
fifteen

16 sedici
SEH-dee-chee
sixteen

17 diciassette
dee-chah-SEH-teh
seventeen

18 diciotto
dee-CHOH-toh
eighteen

19 diciannove
dee-chah-NOH-veh
nineteen

FUN LANGUAGE FACT: Did you notice that the numbers 11 through 19 all have "dici" in them—sometimes at the end of the word and sometimes at the front? This comes from the word **dieci**, or *ten*.

5

Scan here to hear the words!

I numeri (Numbers)
ee NOO-meh-ree

20
venti
VEHN-tee
twenty

30
trenta
TREHN-tah
thirty

40
quaranta
kwah-RAHN-tah
forty

50
cinquanta
cheen-KWAHN-tah
fifty

60
sessanta
seh-SAHN-tah
sixty

70
settanta
seh-TAHN-tah
seventy

80
ottanta
oh-TAHN-tah
eighty

90
novanta
noh-VAHN-tah
ninety

100
cento
CHEHN-toh
one hundred

I colori (Colors)
ee koh-LOH-ree

Scan here to hear the words!

rosso
ROH-soh
red

viola
vee-OH-lah
purple

arancione
ah-rahn-CHOH-neh
orange

giallo
JAH-loh
yellow

FUN LANGUAGE FACT:
Giallo is also the word for a mystery or detective story. In 1929, a publishing house in Italy put out a series of detective novels with bright yellow covers, and these kinds of stories have been called "yellows" ever since.

grigio
GREE-joh
gray

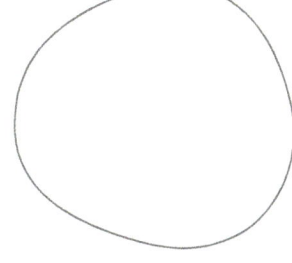

bianco
BYAHN-koh
white

nero
NEH-roh
black

Scan here to hear the words!

I colori (Colors)
ee koh-LOH-ree

rosa
ROH-zah

pink

blu
bloo

blue

verde
VEHR-deh

green

azzurro
ah-DZOO-roh

light blue

FUN LANGUAGE FACT:
Light blue has its own word in Italian, **azzuro**. But in general, you can use **chiaro** and **scuro** to describe *light* and *dark* colors, like **verde chiaro** (*light green*) and **marrone scuro** (*dark brown*).

marrone
mah-ROH-neh

brown

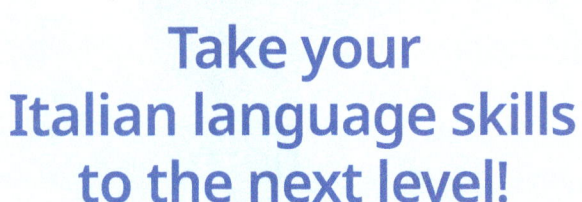

Take your Italian language skills to the next level!

Sign up for RosettaStone.com.

Le forme (Shapes)
leh FOHR-meh

Scan here to hear the words!

il quadrato
eel kwah-DRAH-toh
square

il rettangolo
eel reh-TAHN-goh-loh
rectangle

il cerchio
eel CHEHR-kyoh
circle

l'ovale (m.)
loh-VAH-leh
oval

il triangolo
eel tree-AHN-goh-loh
triangle

la stella
lah STEH-lah
star

il cuore
eel KWOH-reh
heart

il rombo
eel ROHM-boh
diamond

FUN LANGUAGE FACT:
In Italian, you use the word **rombo** to talk about a diamond shape, and **diamante** for the kind of diamond you find in jewelry.

Gli animali (Animals)
lee ah-nee-MAH-lee

il gatto
eel GAH-toh
cat

il cane
eel KAH-neh
dog

l'uccello (m.)
loo-CHEH-loh
bird

FUN LANGUAGE FACT:
The word for *chicken* in Italian is **pollo**. This is also the term used to refer to chicken meat.

la gallina
lah gah-LEE-nah
hen

il gallo
eel GAH-loh
rooster

il coniglio
eel koh-NEE-lyoh
rabbit

il criceto
eel kree-CHEH-toh
hamster

FUN LANGUAGE FACT:
Different languages have different sounds for animals. For example, a rooster says **Chicchirichì!** in Italian but **Cock-a-doodle-doo!** in English. Scan the QR code to hear more Italian animal sounds!

Scan here to hear the words!

la mucca
lah MOO-kah
cow

la pecora
lah PEH-koh-rah
sheep

il maiale
eel mah-YAH-leh
pig

il cavallo
eel kah-VAH-loh
horse

la capra
lah KAH-prah
goat

l'anatra (f.)
LAH-nah-trah
duck

l'oca (f.)
LOH-kah
goose

il tacchino
eel tah-KEE-noh
turkey

la volpe
lah VOHL-peh
fox

Gli animali (Animals)
lee ah-nee-MAH-lee

la rana
lah RAH-nah
frog

il cervo
eel CHEHR-voh
deer

il topo
eel TOH-poh
mouse

il serpente
eel sehr-PEHN-teh
snake

il gufo
eel GOO-foh
owl

lo scoiattolo
loh skoh-YAH-toh-loh
squirrel

il lupo
eel LOO-poh
wolf

FUN LANGUAGE FACT:
While the phrase **in bocca al lupo** (literally, *in the mouth of the wolf*) seems to describe a bad situation, the expression is actually used to wish someone good luck, kind of like *break a leg* in English!

l'orso (m.)
LOHR-soh
bear

Scan here to hear the words!

la tartaruga
lah tahr-tah-ROO-gah
turtle

il riccio
eel REE-choh
hedgehog

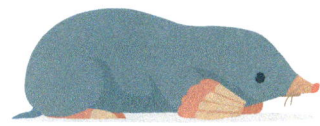

la talpa
lah TAHL-pah
mole

il procione
eel proh-CHOH-neh
raccoon

la puzzola
lah POO-tsoh-lah
skunk

FUN LANGUAGE FACT:
The word **puzzola** comes from **puzza**, which means *bad smell* or *stink*. That makes sense for an animal known for its smell!

il leone
eel leh-OH-neh
lion

la zebra
lah DZEH-brah
zebra

la scimmia
lah SHEE-myah
monkey

Gli animali (Animals)
lee ah-nee-MAH-lee

il gorilla
eel goh-REE-lah
gorilla

la tigre
lah TEE-greh
tiger

il rinoceronte
eel ree-noh-cheh-ROHN-teh
rhinoceros

l'elefante (m.)
leh-leh-FAHN-teh
elephant

FUN LANGUAGE FACT:
Avere una memoria da elefante (literally, *to have the memory of an elephant*) means to be able to remember things very well, like the expression *an elephant never forgets* in English.

il pipistrello
eel pee-pee-STREH-loh
bat

l'ippopotamo (m.)
lee-poh-POH-tah-moh
hippopotamus

il fenicottero
eel feh-nee-KOH-teh-roh
flamingo

la giraffa
lah jee-RAH-fah
giraffe

Scan here to hear the words!

il panda
eel PAHN-dah
panda

il koala
eel koh-AH-lah
koala

il cammello
eel kah-MEH-loh
camel

il canguro
eel kahn-GOO-roh
kangaroo

il pappagallo
eel pah-pah-GAH-loh
parrot

il pinguino
eel peen-GWEE-noh
penguin

il coccodrillo
eel koh-koh-DREE-loh
crocodile

il pesce
eel PEH-sheh
fish

FUN LANGUAGE FACT: The expression **essere sano come un pesce** literally means *to be as healthy as a fish*. It's kind of like *fit as a fiddle* or *healthy as a horse* in English.

Gli animali (Animals)
lee ah-nee-MAH-lee

lo squalo
loh SKWAH-loh
shark

la balena
lah bah-LEH-nah
whale

il delfino
eel dehl-FEE-noh
dolphin

il granchio
eel GRAHN-kyoh
crab

FUN LANGUAGE FACT:
Prendere un granchio (literally, *to catch a crab*) means to make a mistake. This expression comes from fishing, when a tug on the line feels like a big fish but ends up being a crab! Another related Italian expression about confusing two things that are very different is **prendere lucciole per lanterne**, or *taking fireflies for lanterns*.

il polpo
eel POHL-poh
octopus

il cavalluccio marino
eel kah-vah-LOO-choh mah-REE-noh
seahorse

l'aragosta (f.)
lah-rah-GOH-stah
lobster

Scan here to hear the words!

la stella marina
lah STEH-lah mah-REE-nah
sea star

la foca
lah FOH-kah
seal

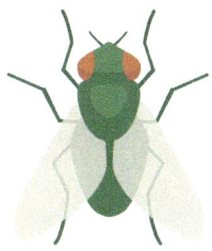

la mosca
lah MOHS-kah
fly

la farfalla
lah fahr-FAH-lah
butterfly

la falena
lah fah-LEH-nah
moth

il bruco
eel BROO-koh
caterpillar

la lucciola
lah LOO-choh-lah
firefly

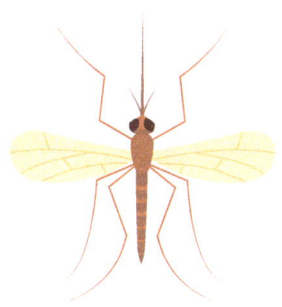

la zanzara
lah dzahn-DZAH-rah
mosquito

la coccinella
lah koh-chee-NEH-lah
ladybug

17

Scan here to hear the words!

Gli animali (Animals)
lee ah-nee-MAH-lee

l'ape (f.)
LAH-peh
bee

FUN LANGUAGE FACT: A person who is **come una formica** (literally, *like an ant*) is very hard-working—kind of like being *busy as a bee* in English!

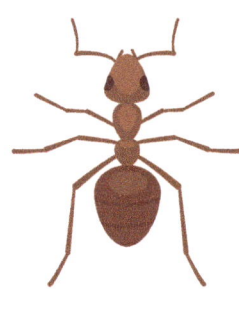

la formica
lah fohr-MEE-kah
ant

il ragno
eel RAH-nyoh
spider

la cavalletta
lah kah-vah-LEH-tah
grasshopper

lo scarabeo
loh skah-rah-BEH-oh
beetle

il verme
eel VEHR-meh
worm

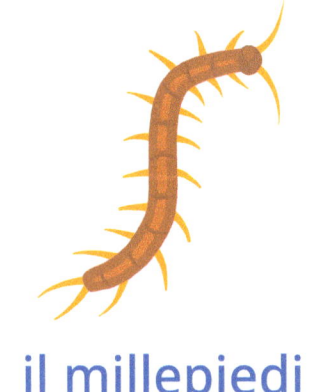

il millepiedi
eel mee-leh-PYEH-dee
centipede

FUN LANGUAGE FACT: **Millepiedi** literally means *thousand feet* in Italian.

Frutta e verdura
(Fruits and vegetables)
FROO-tah eh vehr-DOO-rah

Scan here to hear the words!

la mela
lah MEH-lah
apple

FUN LANGUAGE FACT:
The phrase **l'altra metà della mela** (literally, *the other half of the apple*) refers to a loved one. Calling someone **l'altra metà della mela** is like saying, *you're my other half*!

la banana
lah bah-NAH-nah
banana

l'arancia (f.)
lah-RAHN-chah
orange

la fragola
lah FRAH-goh-lah
strawberry

il mango
eel MAHN-goh
mango

FUN LANGUAGE FACT:
Pesca is also the Italian word for *fishing*.

la pesca
lah PEH-skah
peach

19

Frutta e verdura
(Fruits and vegetables)
FROO-tah eh vehr-DOO-rah

la pera
lah PEH-rah
pear

il pompelmo
eel pohm-PEHL-moh
grapefruit

l'albicocca (f.)
lahl-bee-KOH-kah
apricot

l'uva (f.)
LOO-vah
grapes

FUN LANGUAGE FACT:
Did you know that a raisin is a dried grape? The word **uvetta** in Italian literally means *little grape*.

l'uvetta (f.)
loo-VEH-tah
raisins

la susina
lah soo-ZEE-nah
plum

la prugna secca
lah PROO-nyah SEH-kah
prune

FUN LANGUAGE FACT:
Prugna is another word for *plum*, and **secca** means *dried*, so **prugna secca** literally means *dried plum*.

Scan here to hear the words!

il fico
eel FEE-koh
fig

la mora
lah MOH-rah
blackberry

il mirtillo
eel meer-TEE-loh
blueberry

il mirtillo rosso
eel meer-TEE-loh ROH-soh
cranberry

il lampone
eel lahm-POH-neh
raspberry

il ribes nero
eel REE-behs NEH-roh
black currant

il limone
eel lee-MOH-neh
lemon

la limetta
lah lee-MEH-tah
lime

la ciliegia
lah chee-LYEH-jah
cherry

Frutta e verdura
(Fruits and vegetables)
FROO-tah eh vehr-DOO-rah

il melone
eel meh-LOH-neh
melon

l'anguria (f.)
lahn-GOO-ryah
watermelon

FUN LANGUAGE FACT: Another common word for *watermelon* is **cocomero**. The word that people use depends on where they live in Italy.

il kiwi
eel KEE-wee
kiwi

l'ananas (m.)
LAH-nah-nahs
pineapple

la papaya
lah pah-PAH-yah
papaya

la guava
la GWAH-vah
guava

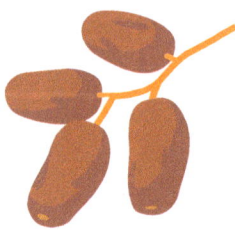

il dattero
eel DAH-teh-roh
date

il frutto della passione
eel FROO-toh DEH-lah pah-SYOH-neh
passion fruit

Scan here to hear the words!

il caco
eel KAH-koh
persimmon

la noce di cocco
lah NOH-cheh dee KOH-koh
coconut

l'oliva (f.)
loh-LEE-vah
olive

il cetriolo
eel cheh-tree-OH-loh
cucumber

i broccoli
ee BROH-koh-lee
broccoli

la melanzana
lah meh-lahn-TSAH-nah
eggplant

il peperone
eel peh-peh-ROH-neh
bell pepper

FUN LANGUAGE FACT:
Watch out! If you order a "pepperoni" pizza in Italy, you might get it with *bell peppers*, or **peperoni**! If you want pizza with *spicy salami*, ask for **salamino piccante** as a topping instead. The name of this type of pizza is often **pizza diavola**, or *devil pizza*.

Frutta e verdura
(Fruits and vegetables)
FROO-tah eh vehr-DOO-rah

i piselli
ee pee-ZEH-lee
peas

il pomodoro
eel poh-moh-DOH-roh
tomato

FUN LANGUAGE FACT:
Pomodoro literally means *golden apple*. When tomatoes were introduced to Italy in the sixteenth century, they were small and yellow, like golden apples.

la carota
lah kah-ROH-tah
carrot

gli spinaci
lee spee-NAH-chee
spinach

la lattuga
lah lah-TOO-gah
lettuce

il mais
eel MAH-ees
corn

FUN LANGUAGE FACT:
The Italian word **mais** comes from the Spanish word for corn ("maíz"). An older word for *corn* in Italian is **granoturco**, which literally means *Turkish grain* or *Turkish wheat*.

Scan here to hear the words!

l'indivia (f.)
leen-DEE-vyah
endive

il cavolfiore
eel kah-vohl-FYOH-reh
cauliflower

il cavolo
eel KAH-voh-loh
cabbage

i cavoletti di Bruxelles
ee kah-voh-LEH-tee dee brook-SEHL
Brussels sprouts

FUN LANGUAGE FACT:
Did you notice? Cauliflower and Brussels sprouts are both different kinds of **cavolo**, or *cabbage*, in Italian.

la verza
lah VEHR-dzah
kale

la cipolla
lah chee-POH-lah
onion

i fagiolini
ee fah-joh-LEE-nee
green beans

il carciofo
eel kahr-CHOH-foh
artichoke

Frutta e verdura
(Fruits and vegetables)
FROO-tah eh vehr-DOO-rah

la pastinaca
lah pah-stee-NAH-kah
parsnip

la patata
lah pah-TAH-tah
potato

la patata dolce
lah pah-TAH-tah DOHL-cheh
sweet potato

il ravanello
eel rah-vah-NEH-loh
radish

il porro
eel POH-roh
leek

la zucchina
lah dzoo-KEE-nah
zucchini

la zucca
lah DZOO-kah
pumpkin

FUN LANGUAGE FACTS:
Because of the shape of pumpkins, the word **zucca** is often used in Italian expressions to refer to someone's head or mind. For example, **avere sale in zucca** (literally, *to have salt in the pumpkin*) means *to be smart*. It is similar to the English expression *to have one's head on straight*.

Scan here to hear the words!

il fungo
eel FOON-goh
mushroom

l'asparago (m.)
lah-SPAH-rah-goh
asparagus

l'avocado (m.)
lah-voh-KAH-doh
avocado

l'aglio (m.)
LAH-lyoh
garlic

lo scalogno
loh skah-LOH-nyoh
shallot

il sedano
eel SEH-dah-noh
celery

lo zenzero
loh DZEHN-dzeh-roh
ginger

Take your
Italian language skills
to the next level!

Sign up for
RosettaStone.com.

Scan here to hear the words!

Le noci (Nuts)
leh NOH-chee

la noce
lah NOH-cheh
walnut

la nocciola
lah noh-CHOH-lah
hazelnut

il pistacchio
eel pee-STAH-kyoh
pistachio

l'arachide (f.)
lah-RAH-kee-deh
peanut

FUN LANGUAGE FACT:
Another name for a *peanut* is **nocciolina americana**.

la mandorla
lah MAHN-dohr-lah
almond

la noce pecan
lah NOH-cheh peh-KAHN
pecan

l'anacardo (m.)
lah-nah-KAHR-doh
cashew

la castagna
lah kahs-TAH-nyah
chestnut

Il cibo (Food)
eel CHEE-boh

Scan here to hear the words!

l'uovo (m.)
LWOH-voh
egg

FUN LANGUAGE FACT: The Italian name for a *sunny-side-up egg* is **uovo all'occhio di bue**, which literally means *ox eye egg*—probably because this breakfast dish looks a bit like an eye!

il burro
eel BOO-roh
butter

lo yogurt
loh YOH-goort
yogurt

la marmellata
lah mahr-meh-LAH-tah
jam

il miele
eel MYEH-leh
honey

FUN LANGUAGE FACT: The expression **buono come il pane** (literally, *good as bread*) is used to describe a kind and good-natured person.

il pane
eel PAH-neh
bread

i cereali
ee cheh-reh-AH-lee
cereal

Il cibo (Food)
eel CHEE-boh

la farina d'avena
lah fah-REE-nah dah-VEH-nah
oatmeal

il formaggio
eel fohr-MAH-joh
cheese

il panino
eel pah-NEE-noh
sandwich

la zuppa
lah TSOO-pah
soup

FUN LANGUAGE FACT:
Another word often used for *soup* is **minestra**. **Zuppa** is usually a simple broth with vegetables but without pasta or rice, while **minestra** usually includes pasta and rice. **Minestrone**, a soup enjoyed worldwide, literally means *big soup* and is thick with vegetables and rice or pasta.

l'insalata (f.)
leen-sah-LAH-tah
salad

la pasta
lah PAHS-tah
pasta

il riso
eel REE-zoh
rice

Scan here to hear the words!

le lenticchie
leh lehn-TEE-kyeh
lentils

i fagioli
ee fah-JOH-lee
beans

FUN LANGUAGE FACT:
If an event **capita a fagiolo**, or *happens at the bean*, it happens just in time, at the perfect moment.

la farina
lah fah-REE-nah
flour

il grano
eel GRAH-noh
wheat

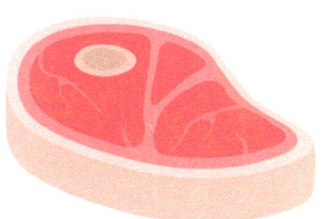

la carne
lah KAHR-neh
meat

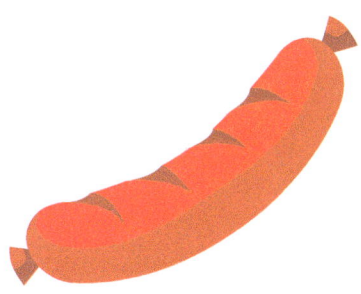

la salsiccia
lah sahl-SEE-chah
sausage

FUN LANGUAGE FACT:
There are many variations of sausage across the regions of Italy, both in type and in name! Some of the names used across the country to refer to *sausage* are **luganega**, **salamella**, **salamina**, **salamino**, **salametto**, **bardiccio**, **rocchio**, and **zazzicchia**.

il salame
eel sah-LAH-meh
salami

31

Il cibo (Food)
eel CHEE-boh

il prosciutto
eel proh-SHOO-toh
ham

FUN LANGUAGE FACT:
The expression **avere il prosciutto sugli occhi** (literally, *to have ham on the eyes*) means to not be able to notice or accept something obvious.

il tonno
eel TOH-noh
tuna

i germogli di soia
ee jehr-MOH-lee dee SOH-yah
soybeans

le patate fritte
leh pah-TAH-teh FREE-teh
fries

l'olio (m.)
LOH-lyoh
oil

l'aceto (m.)
lah-CHEH-toh
vinegar

la senape
lah SEH-nah-peh
mustard

FUN LANGUAGE FACT:
If a situation is described as **liscio come l'olio** (literally, *smooth as oil*), it means that it's going smoothly, without any complications.

Scan here to hear the words!

il sale
eel SAH-leh
salt

il pepe
eel PEH-peh
pepper

FUN LANGUAGE FACT:
A person described as **tutto pepe**, or *all pepper*, is cheerful, energetic, and fun to be around!

le spezie
leh SPEH-tsyeh
spices

le erbe aromatiche
leh EHR-beh ah-roh-MAH-tee-keh
herbs

lo zucchero
loh TSOO-keh-roh
sugar

le caramelle
leh kah-rah-MEH-leh
candy

FUN LANGUAGE FACT:
Outside of Italy, *gelato* refers to a specific kind of Italian ice cream, but in Italian, it is the general word for **ice cream**.

il gelato
eel jeh-LAH-toh
ice cream

Scan here to hear the words!

Il cibo (Food)
eel CHEE-boh

la crostata
lah kroh-STAH-tah
pie

FUN LANGUAGE FACT:
There is no perfect Italian translation of *pie*. Two words that come close are **torta**, which is more like *cake*, and **crostata**, which is often translated as *tart*. So *apple pie* can be translated as either **torta di mele** or **crostata di mele**, depending on what the pie looks like!

la torta
lah TOHR-tah
cake

il biscotto
eel bee-SKOH-toh
cookie

il cioccolato
eel choh-koh-LAH-toh
chocolate

le cialde
leh CHAHL-deh
waffles

FUN LANGUAGE FACT:
Along with **cialda**, the English word *waffle* is also often used to talk about this food.

la panna montata
lah PAH-nah mohn-TAH-tah
whipped cream

34

Le bevande (Drinks)
leh beh-VAHN-deh

Scan here to hear the words!

l'acqua (f.)
LAH-kwah
water

l'acqua frizzante (f.)
LAH-kwah free-DZAHN-teh
sparkling water

la bibita
lah BEE-bee-tah
soda

il tè
eel teh
tea

il caffè
eel kah-FEH
coffee

FUN LANGUAGE FACT: There are more than forty types of coffee in Italy. Many people know about the **espresso** and the **cappuccino**, but other popular examples are the **nutellino** (made with Nutella hazelnut cocoa spread) and **caffè d'orzo** (made from barley).

la cioccolata calda
lah choh-koh-LAH-tah KAHL-dah
hot chocolate

il latte
eel LAH-teh
milk

il succo di frutta
eel SOO-koh dee FROO-tah
juice

I mezzi di trasporto (Transportation)
ee MEH-dzee dee trahs-POHR-toh

la macchina
lah MAH-kee-nah
car

FUN LANGUAGE FACT:
Another word for *car* is **l'auto**.

il taxi
eel TAHK-see
taxi

il furgoncino
eel foor-gohn-CHEE-noh
van

il camion
eel KAH-myohn
truck

il camion dei pompieri
eel KAH-myohn dey pohm-PYEH-ree
fire engine

FUN LANGUAGE FACT:
Camion is used for a large truck that transports goods and people, while **pick-up** is often used for a small pickup truck. The word for *fire engine*, **camion dei pompieri**, literally means *truck of the firefighters*, and **camion delle immondizie** literally means *truck of the garbage*.

il camion delle immondizie
eel KAH-myohn deh-leh ee-mohn-DEE-tsyeh
garbage truck

Scan here to hear the words!

l'auto della polizia (f.)
LOW-toh deh-lah poh-lee-TSEE-ah
police car

FUN LANGUAGE FACT:
The Italian police car is nicknamed **Pantera**, or *Panther*. This name was first given to older models of police cars in Italy, which were black and very fast. Even when the color of Italian police cars changed to blue and white, the nickname remained.

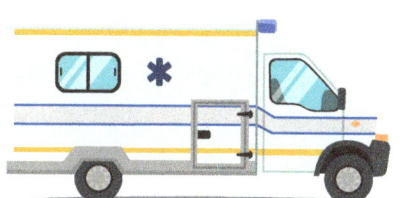

l'ambulanza (f.)
lahm-boo-LAHN-tsah
ambulance

la bicicletta
lah bee-chee-KLEH-tah
bicycle

il monopattino
eel moh-noh-PAH-tee-noh
scooter

la motocicletta
lah moh-toh-chee-KLEH-tah
motorcycle

il treno
eel TREH-noh
train

la metropolitana
lah meh-troh-poh-lee-TAH-nah
subway

37

Scan here to hear the words!

I mezzi di trasporto
(Transportation)
ee MEH-dzee dee trahs-POHR-toh

l'autobus (m.)
LOW-toh-boos
bus

la scavatrice
lah skah-vah-TREE-cheh
digger

il traghetto
eel trah-GEH-toh
ferry

la barca
lah BAHR-kah
boat

la barca a vela
lah BAHR-kah ah VEH-lah
sailboat

la nave
lah NAH-veh
ship

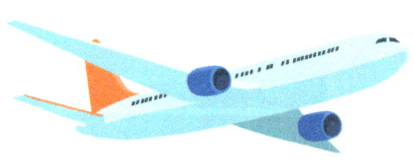

l'aeroplano (m.)
lie-roh-PLAH-noh
plane

l'elicottero (m.)
leh-lee-KOH-teh-roh
helicopter

la mongolfiera
lah mohn-gohl-FYEH-rah
hot-air balloon

Abiti ed accessori
(Clothing and accessories)
AH-bee-tee ehd ah-cheh-SOH-ree

Scan here to hear the words!

la camicia
lah kah-MEE-chah
shirt

la camicetta
lah kah-mee-CHEH-tah
blouse

la maglietta
lah mah-LYEH-tah
T-shirt

il cardigan
eel KAHR-dee-gahn
cardigan

il maglione
eel mah-LYOH-neh
sweater

i pantaloni
ee pahn-tah-LOH-nee
pants

l'abito (m.)
LAH-bee-toh
dress

la gonna
lah GOH-nah
skirt

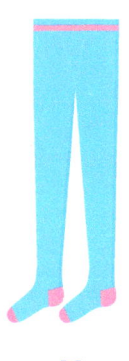

i collant
ee koh-LAHN
tights

39

Abiti ed accessori
(Clothing and accessories)
AH-bee-tee ehd ah-cheh-SOH-ree

i pantaloncini corti
ee pahn-tah-lohn-CHEE-nee KOHR-tee
shorts

i jeans
ee jeens
jeans

i calzini
ee kahl-TSEE-nee
socks

il cappotto
eel kah-POH-toh
coat

l'impermeabile (m.)
leem-pehr-meh-AH-bee-leh
raincoat

la giacca
lah JAH-kah
jacket

il cappello
eel kah-PEH-loh
hat

FUN LANGUAGE FACT:
Watch out! **Cappello**, the Italian word for *hat*, is very similar to **capello**, the word for a *strand of hair*.

il cappellino da baseball
eel kah-peh-LEE-noh dah BEYS-bohl
baseball cap

Scan here to hear the words!

gli orecchini
lee oh-reh-KEE-nee
earrings

il braccialetto
eel brah-chah-LEH-toh
bracelet

la collana
lah koh-LAH-nah
necklace

l'anello (m.)
lah-NEH-loh
ring

i guanti
ee GWAHN-tee
gloves

la sciarpa
lah SHAHR-pah
scarf

la cintura
lah cheen-TOO-rah
belt

gli occhiali da sole
lee oh-KYAH-lee dah SOH-leh
sunglasses

il costume da bagno
eel kohs-TOO-meh dah BAH-nyoh
bathing suit

41

Scan here to hear the words!

Abiti ed accessori
(Clothing and accessories)
AH-bee-tee ehd ah-cheh-SOH-ree

il farfallino
eel fahr-fah-LEE-noh
bow tie

il gilet
eel jee-LEH
vest

FUN LANGUAGE FACT:
While **gilet** comes from the French word for *vest*, another Italian word for it is **panciotto**.

FUN LANGUAGE FACT:
Farfallino literally means *little butterfly*, probably because of the shape of a bow tie. Another word for *bow tie* is **papillon**, which means *butterfly* in French.

la cravatta
lah krah-VAH-tah
tie

il completo
eel kohm-PLEH-toh
suit

gli occhiali da vista
lee oh-KYAH-lee dah VEE-stah
glasses

il pigiama
eel pee-JAH-mah
pajamas

l'abbigliamento intimo (m.)
lah-bee-lyah-MEHN-toh EEN-tee-moh
underwear

Le scarpe (Shoes)
leh SKAHR-peh

Scan here to hear the words!

i sandali
ee SAHN-dah-lee
sandals

le infradito
leh een-frah-DEE-toh
flip-flops

i tacchi alti
ee TAH-kee AHL-tee
high heels

gli stivali
lee stee-VAH-lee
boots

gli stivali da pioggia
lee stee-VAH-lee dah PYOH-jah
rain boots

le scarpe da ginnastica
leh SKAHR-peh dah jee-NAHS-tee-kah
sneakers

le pantofole
leh pahn-TOH-foh-leh
slippers

FUN LANGUAGE FACT:
The word **pantofolaio** is often used to refer to a person who loves to spend time at home, especially resting on the couch—kind of like *couch potato* in English.

43

Il corpo (The body)
eel KOHR-poh

la testa
lah TEHS-tah
head

il viso
eel VEE-zoh
face

l'occhio (m.)
LOH-kyoh
eye

l'orecchio (m.)
loh-REH-kyoh
ear

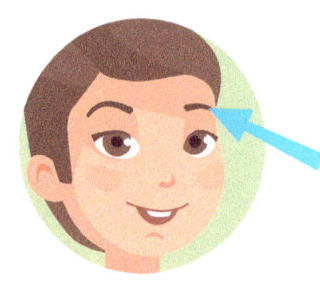

il sopracciglio
eel soh-prah-CHEE-lyoh
eyebrow

FUN LANGUAGE FACT:
The word **sopracciglio** is made up of the words **sopra** (*above*) and **ciglio** (*eyelash*).

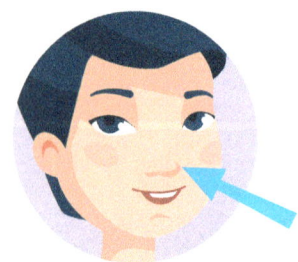

il naso
eel NAH-zoh
nose

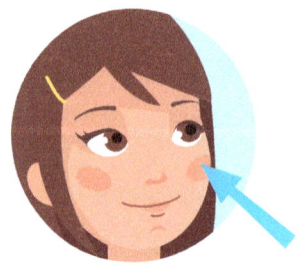

la guancia
lah GWAHN-chah
cheek

il mento
eel MEHN-toh
chin

Scan here to hear the words!

la bocca
lah BOH-kah
mouth

FUN LANGUAGE FACT:
The expression **acqua in bocca** (literally, *water in the mouth*) is used when asking someone to keep a secret.

le labbra
leh LAH-brah
lips

i denti
ee DEHN-tee
teeth

i capelli
ee kah-PEH-lee
hair

FUN LANGUAGE FACT:
Capelli, the word for *hair*, is plural. **Un capello** would refer to just one *strand of hair*.

le spalle
leh SPAH-leh
shoulders

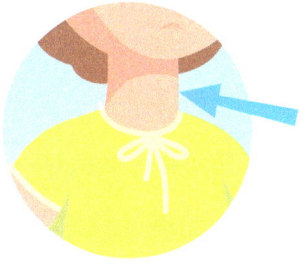

il collo
eel KOH-loh
neck

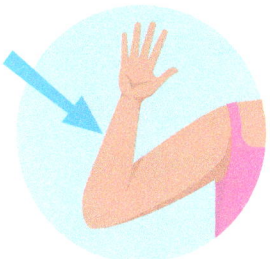

il braccio
eel BRAH-choh
arm

Il corpo (The body)
eel KOHR-poh

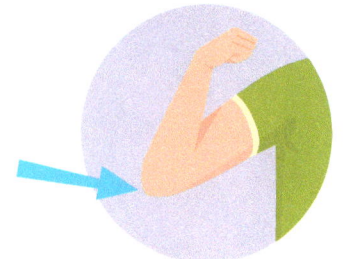

il gomito
eel GOH-mee-toh
elbow

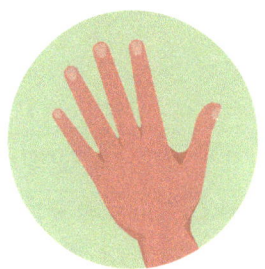

la mano
lah MAH-noh
hand

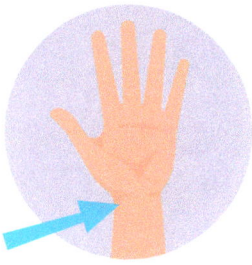

il polso
eel POHL-soh
wrist

il dito
eel DEE-toh
finger

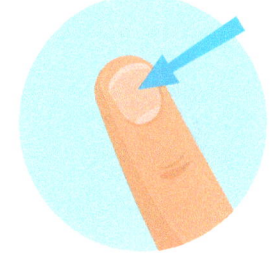

l'unghia (f.)
LOON-gyah
fingernail

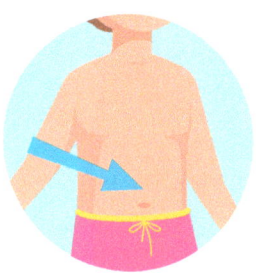

la pancia
lah PAHN-chah
tummy

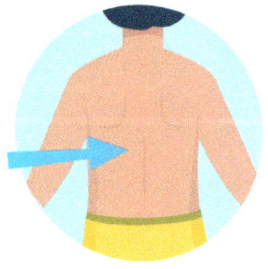

la schiena
lah SKYEH-nah
back

i fianchi
ee FYAHN-kee
hips

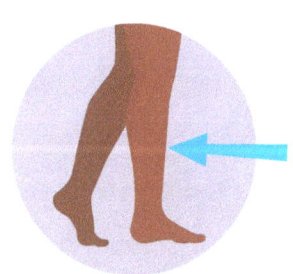

la gamba
lah GAHM-bah
leg

Scan here to hear the words!

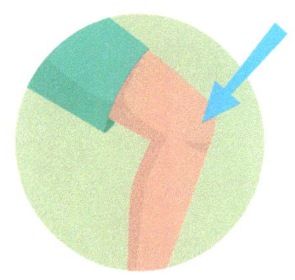

il ginocchio
eel jee-NOH-kyoh
knee

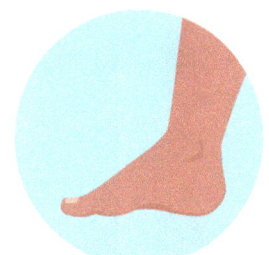

il piede
eel PYEH-deh
foot

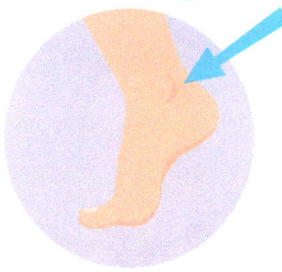

la caviglia
lah kah-VEE-lyah
ankle

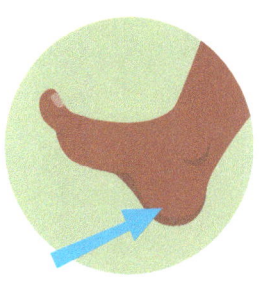

il tallone
eel tah-LOH-neh
heel

FUN LANGUAGE FACT:
The expression **andarci con i piedi di piombo** (literally, *to go there with feet of lead*) means *to do something very cautiously*. An English expression that sounds like the opposite but has a similar meaning is *to tread lightly*.

le dita dei piedi
leh DEE-tah dey PYEH-dee
toes

FUN LANGUAGE FACT:
Le dita dei piedi literally means *the fingers of the feet*.

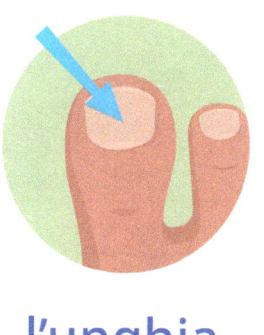

l'unghia
LOON-gyah
toenail

47

La famiglia (Family)
lah fah-MEE-lyah

la mamma
lah MAH-mah
mom

il papà
eel pah-PAH
dad

i genitori
ee jeh-nee-TOH-ree
parents

la figlia
lah FEE-lyah
daughter

il figlio
eel FEE-lyoh
son

la sorella
lah soh-REH-lah
sister

il fratello
eel frah-TEH-loh
brother

la nonna
lah NOH-nah
grandmother

il nonno
eel NOH-noh
grandfather

Scan here to hear the words!

lo zio
loh TSEE-oh
uncle

la zia
lah TSEE-ah
aunt

il cugino
eel koo-JEE-noh
cousin (male)

la cugina
lah koo-JEE-nah
cousin (female)

il bebè
eel beh-BEH
baby

il nipote
eel nee-POH-teh
grandson

la nipote
lah nee-POH-teh
granddaughter

FUN LANGUAGE FACT:
While there are different words in English for *grandson*, *granddaughter*, *nephew*, and *niece*, the Italian word **nipote** can refer to any of them. Usually the context can help you figure out which family members are being discussed!

49

A casa (At home)
ah KAH-zah

l'appartamento (m.)
lah-pahr-tah-MEHN-toh
apartment

le scale
leh SKAH-leh
stairs

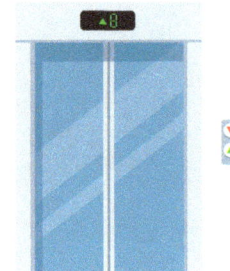

l'ascensore (m.)
lah-shehn-SOH-reh
elevator

il tetto
eel TEH-toh
roof

il balcone
eel bahl-KOH-neh
balcony

l'ingresso (m.)
leen-GREH-soh
hallway

la finestra
lah fee-NEHS-trah
window

la porta
lah POHR-tah
door

FUN LANGUAGE FACT:
La porta can also refer to the *net* or *goal* in sports.

Scan here to hear the words!

la stanza
lah STAHN-tsah
room

il divano
eel dee-VAH-noh
couch

FUN LANGUAGE FACT:
A couch can also be called **un sofà**, like *sofa* in English.

la moquette
lah moh-KEH-tuh
carpet

FUN LANGUAGE FACT:
La moquette, the word for a *wall-to-wall carpet*, comes from French.

il tappeto
eel tah-PEH-toh
rug

il pavimento
eel pah-vee-MEHN-toh
floor

la poltrona
lah pohl-TROH-nah
armchair

lo scaffale
loh skah-FAH-leh
shelf

A casa (At home)
ah KAH-zah

il tavolo
eel TAH-voh-loh
table

FUN LANGUAGE FACT:
While **il tavolo** can refer to any kind of table, **la tavola** is specifically a table that is set for a meal. The word **tavola** can also mean *board*, so **una tavola da surf** is a *surfboard*!

il tavolino
eel tah-voh-LEE-noh
coffee table

la sedia
lah SEH-dyah
chair

la scrivania
lah skree-vah-NEE-ah
desk

il computer
eel kohm-PYOO-tehr
computer

la libreria
lah lee-breh-REE-ah
bookcase

FUN LANGUAGE FACT:
La libreria can also refer to a *bookstore*. The word for *library*, however, is **la biblioteca**.

Scan here to hear the words!

il cellulare
eel cheh-loo-LAH-reh
cell phone

la lampada
lah LAHM-pah-dah
lamp

il quadro
eel KWAH-droh
painting

la televisione
lah teh-leh-vee-ZYOH-neh
television

il letto
eel LEH-toh
bed

il cuscino
eel koo-SHEE-noh
pillow

la cassettiera
lah kah-seh-TYEH-rah
dresser

l'orologio (m.)
loh-roh-LOH-joh
clock

FUN LANGUAGE FACT:
L'orologio can also refer to a *wristwatch*.

A casa (At home)
ah KAH-zah

il ventilatore
eel vehn-tee-lah-TOH-reh
fan

il vaso
eel VAH-zoh
vase

la tenda
lah TEHN-dah
curtain

i giocattoli
ee joh-KAH-toh-lee
toys

il giardino
eel jahr-DEE-noh
garden

l'attico (m.)
LAH-tee-koh
attic

la cantina
lah kahn-TEE-nah
basement

la lavatrice
lah lah-vah-TREE-cheh
washer

l'asciugatrice (f.)
lah-shoo-gah-TREE-cheh
dryer

In cucina (In the kitchen)
een koo-CHEE-nah

Scan here to hear the words!

il fornello
eel fohr-NEH-loh
stove

FUN LANGUAGE FACT:
The word **cucina** could refer to a *kitchen*, a *stove*, or a *cuisine* (a specific style of cooking).

il forno
eel FOHR-noh
oven

la pattumiera
lah pah-too-MYEH-rah
garbage can

la pentola
lah PEHN-toh-lah
pot

la padella
lah pah-DEH-lah
pan

la lavastoviglie
lah lah-vah-stoh-VEE-lyeh
dishwasher

il microonde
eel mee-kroh-OHN-deh
microwave

il tostapane
eel tohs-tah-PAH-neh
toaster

Scan here to hear the words!

In cucina (In the kitchen)
een koo-CHEE-nah

la teiera
lah teh-YEH-rah
tea kettle

il grembiule
eel grehm-BYOO-leh
apron

il frullatore
eel froo-lah-TOH-reh
blender

il frigorifero
eel free-goh-REE-feh-roh
refrigerator

FUN LANGUAGE FACT:
Il frigorifero can be shortened to **il frigo**, just like *refrigerator* can be shortened to *fridge*.

il congelatore
eel kohn-jeh-lah-TOH-reh
freezer

il rubinetto
eel roo-bee-NEH-toh
faucet

il lavello
eel lah-VEH-loh
kitchen sink

FUN LANGUAGE FACT:
The word **lavandino** can refer to either a *kitchen sink* or a *bathroom sink*. However, **lavello** often refers specifically to a *kitchen sink*, and **lavabo** refers to a *bathroom sink*.

56

A tavola (At the table)
ah TAH-voh-lah

Scan here to hear the words!

la forchetta
lah fohr-KEH-tah
fork

il coltello
eel kohl-TEH-loh
knife

il cucchiaio
eel koo-KYAH-yoh
spoon

il bicchiere
eel bee-KYEH-reh
glass

il piatto
eel PYAH-toh
plate

la scodella
lah skoh-DEH-lah
bowl

la tazza
lah TAH-tsah
cup

Take your Italian language skills to the next level!

Sign up for RosettaStone.com.

Scan here to hear the words!

A tavola (At the table)
ah TAH-voh-lah

la caraffa
lah kah-RAH-fah
pitcher

il tovagliolo
eel toh-vah-LYOH-loh
napkin

la tovaglia
lah toh-VAH-lyah
tablecloth

i piatti
ee PYAH-tee
dishes

la colazione
lah koh-lah-TSYOH-neh
breakfast

il pranzo
eel PRAHN-dzoh
lunch

la cena
lah CHEH-nah
dinner

il dolce
eel DOHL-cheh
dessert

il menù
eel meh-NOO
menu

Il bagno (Bath time)
eel BAH-nyoh

Scan here to hear the words!

lo spazzolino
loh spah-tsoh-LEE-noh
toothbrush

il dentifricio
eel dehn-tee-FREE-choh
toothpaste

il filo interdentale
eel FEE-loh een-tehr-dehn-TAH-leh
floss

la carta igienica
lah KAHR-tah ee-JEH-nee-kah
toilet paper

la toilette
lah twah-LEH-tuh
toilet

il pettine
eel PEH-tee-neh
comb

la spazzola
lah SPAH-tsoh-lah
hairbrush

la crema per il corpo
lah KREH-mah pehr eel KOHR-poh
lotion

FUN LANGUAGE FACT: Another word that can be used for *lotion* is the more similar **lozione**. The difference is that **crema per il corpo** (literally, *cream for the body*) is creamier or thicker than **lozione**.

Scan here to hear the words!

Il bagno (Bath time)
eel BAH-nyoh

la vasca da bagno
lah VAH-skah dah BAH-nyoh
bathtub

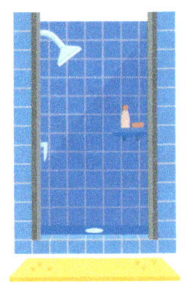
la doccia
lah DOH-chah
shower

l'asciugamano (m.)
lah-shoo-gah-MAH-noh
towel

il sapone
eel sah-POH-neh
soap

lo shampoo
loh SHAHM-poh
shampoo

FUN LANGUAGE FACT:
Asciugare means *to dry*, and **mano** means *hand*, so the word for *towel*, **asciugamano**, literally means what it does: dry hands!

lo specchio
loh SPEH-kyoh
mirror

il lavandino
eel lah-vahn-DEE-noh
sink

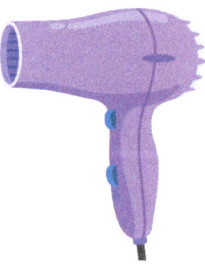
il fon
eel fohn
hair dryer

A scuola (At school)
ah SKWOH-lah

Scan here to hear the words!

il quaderno
eel kwah-DEHR-noh
notebook

le forbici
leh FOHR-bee-chee
scissors

il righello
eel ree-GEH-loh
ruler

la gomma per cancellare
lah GOH-mah pehr kahn-cheh-LAH-reh
eraser

il libro
eel LEE-broh
book

la lavagna
lah lah-VAH-nyah
blackboard

la lavagna magnetica
lah lah-VAH-nyah mah-NYEH-tee-kah
whiteboard

Take your Italian language skills to the next level!

Sign up for RosettaStone.com.

Scan here to hear the words!

A scuola (At school)
ah SKWOH-lah

l'uniforme (f.)
loo-nee-FOHR-meh
uniform

la mensa
lah MEHN-sah
cafeteria

il portapranzo
eel pohr-tah-PRAHN-dzoh
lunch box

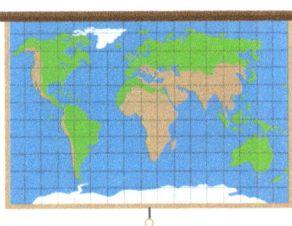

la cartina
lah kahr-TEE-nah
map

la matita
lah mah-TEE-tah
pencil

FUN LANGUAGE FACT:
Portapranzo is made of the words **porta**, which means *brings* or *carries*, and **pranzo**, which means *lunch*. You can also use the term **il pranzo al sacco** (literally, *lunch in a sack*) to refer to a *packed lunch*.

il pastello a cera
eel pahs-TEH-loh ah CHEH-rah
crayon

il pennarello
eel peh-nah-REH-loh
marker

la penna
lah PEH-nah
pen

Lo sport (Sports)
loh spohrt

Scan here to hear the words!

il calcio
eel KAHL-choh
soccer

FUN LANGUAGE FACT: The word **calcio** literally means *kick*, and different kinds of kicks in soccer also use this word. For example, a *kick-off* is **calcio d'inizio** and a *penalty kick* is **calcio di rigore**.

il football americano
eel FOOT-bohl ah-meh-ree-KAH-noh
football

la pallacanestro
lah pah-lah-kah-NEHS-troh
basketball

il tennis
eel TEH-nees
tennis

il baseball
eel BEYS-bohl
baseball

lo sci
loh shee
skiing

il pattinaggio su ghiaccio
eel pah-tee-NAH-joh soo GYAH-choh
ice-skating

il golf
eel gohlf
golf

Lo sport (Sports)
loh spohrt

il ciclismo
eel chee-KLEEZ-moh

cycling

il nuoto
eel NWOH-toh

swimming

le immersioni
leh ee-mehr-SYOH-nee

diving

l'equitazione (f.)
leh-kwee-tah-TSYOH-neh

horseback riding

le escursioni
leh ehs-koor-SYOH-nee

hiking

il canottaggio
eel kah-noh-TAH-joh

rowing

la vela
lah VEH-lah

sailing

fare surf
FAH-reh surf

surfing

la ginnastica artistica
lah jee-NAHS-tee-kah ahr-TEES-tee-kah

gymnastics

Scan here to hear the words!

il ballo
eel BAH-loh
dancing

andare con lo skateboard
ahn-DAH-reh kohn loh SKEYT-bohrd
skateboarding

hockey su ghiaccio
OH-key soo GYAH-choh
ice hockey

la pallavolo
lah pah-lah-VOH-loh
volleyball

la corsa
lah KOHR-sah
running

la lotta
lah LOH-tah
wrestling

il tennis da tavolo
eel TEH-nees dah TAH-voh-loh
table tennis

le arti marziali
leh AHR-tee mahr-TSYAH-lee
martial arts

il tiro con l'arco
eel TEE-roh kohn LAHR-koh
archery

L'attrezzatura per lo sport
(Sports equipment)
lah-treh-tsah-TOO-rah pehr loh spohrt

lo stadio
loh STAH-dyoh
stadium

la porta
lah POHR-tah
goal

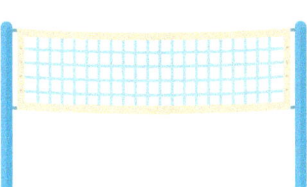

la rete
lah REH-teh
net

il canestro
eel kah-NEHS-troh
basketball hoop

la palla
lah PAH-lah
ball

il casco
eel KAHS-koh
helmet

i pattini da ghiaccio
ee PAH-tee-nee dah GYAH-choh
ice skates

la mazza da baseball
lah MAH-tsah dah BEYS-bohl
baseball bat

la racchetta da tennis
lah rah-KEH-tah dah TEH-nees
tennis racket

Useful phrases
(Frasi utili)

Scan here to hear the words!

Come stai?

Sto bene, e tu?

Hello!
Ciao!
chow

Good morning.
Buongiorno.
bwohn-JOHR-noh

In Italian, some word forms change depending on who is speaking or who is being spoken to. For example, if you're welcoming a man to your house, you would say **benvenuto**. If you're welcoming a woman to your house, you would say **benvenuta**. If you're welcoming more than one person, use **benvenuti** or **benvenute**.

Good afternoon.
Buon pomeriggio.
bwohn poh-meh-REE-joh

Good evening.
Buona sera.
BWOH-nah SEH-rah

Good night.
Buona notte.
BWOH-nah NOH-teh

Hi, my name is...
Ciao, mi chiamo...
chow, mee KYAH-moh

Pleased to meet you.
Piacere di conoscerti.
pyah-CHEH-reh dee koh-NOH-shehr-tee

Welcome.
Benvenuto/
Benvenuta.
*behn-veh-NOO-toh/
behn-veh-NOO-tah*

Goodbye.
Arrivederci.
ah-ree-veh-DEHR-chee

See you later!
A dopo!
ah DOH-poh

While **Come stai?** is used with a friend or family member, **Come sta?** is a more formal version of the question that can be used with a person you don't know as well. You can use **Come state?** if you are talking to a group of people.

How are you?
Come stai?
KOH-meh sty

What's up?
Come va?
KOH-meh vah

67

Scan here to hear the words!

Useful phrases
(Frasi utili)

I'm well, and you?
Sto bene, e tu?
stoh BEH-neh, eh too

Excuse me.
Scusami.
SKOO-zah-mee

I'm sorry.
Mi dispiace.
mee dees-PYAH-cheh

Thank you very much.
Grazie mille.
GRAH-tsyeh MEE-leh

You're welcome.
Prego.
PREH-goh

I don't understand.
Non capisco.
nohn kah-PEE-skoh

Where is the bathroom?
Dov'è il bagno?
doh-VEH eel BAH-nyoh?

Do you speak English?
Parli inglese?
PAHR-lee een-GLEH-zeh

How old are you?
Quanti anni hai?
KWAHN-tee AH-nee eye

I'm __ years old.
Io ho__ anni.
EE-oh oh __ AH-nee

Potresti farci una foto?

Could you take our picture?
Potresti farci una foto?
poh-TREH-stee FAHR-chee OO-nah FOH-toh

Could you help me?
Potresti aiutarmi?
poh-TREH-stee ah-yoo-TAHR-mee

Please
Per favore
pehr fah-VOH-reh

Another way to say *Okay* is **Va bene**. The phrase literally means *It goes well* and can be used as a response to *How's it going?* But it can also be used like *okay* and *alright* in English.

Okay
Ok
OH-key

Yes
Sí
see

No
No
noh

How much does this cost?
Quanto costa?
KWAHN-toh KOHS-tah

Here!
Ecco!
EH-koh

Enjoy your meal!
Buon appetito!
bwohn ah-peh-TEE-toh

English to Italian Word List

A

almond
la mandorla
lah MAHN-dohr-lah

ambulance
l'ambulanza (f.)
lahm-boo-LAHN-tsah

ankle
la caviglia
lah kah-VEE-lyah

ant
la formica
lah fohr-MEE-kah

apartment
l'appartamento (m.)
lah-pahr-tah-MEHN-toh

apple
la mela
lah MEH-lah

apricot
l'albicocca (f.)
lahl-bee-KOH-kah

apron
il grembiule
eel grehm-BYOO-leh

archery
il tiro con l'arco
eel TEE-roh kohn LAHR-koh

arm
il braccio
eel BRAH-choh

armchair
la poltrona
lah pohl-TROH-nah

artichoke
il carciofo
eel kahr-CHOH-foh

asparagus
l'asparago (m.)
lah-SPAH-rah-goh

attic
l'attico (m.)
LAH-tee-koh

aunt
la zia
lah TSEE-ah

avocado
l'avocado (m.)
lah-voh-KAH-doh

B

baby
il bebè
eel beh-BEH

back
la schiena
lah SKYEH-nah

balcony
il balcone
eel bahl-KOH-neh

ball
la palla
lah PAH-lah

banana
la banana
lah bah-NAH-nah

baseball
il baseball
eel BEYS-bohl

baseball bat
la mazza da baseball
lah MAH-tsah dah BEYS-bohl

baseball cap
il cappellino da baseball
eel kah-peh-LEE-noh dah BEYS-bohl

basement
la cantina
lah kahn-TEE-nah

basketball
la pallacanestro
lah pah-lah-kah-NEHS-troh

basketball hoop
il canestro
eel kah-NEHS-troh

bat
il pipistrello
eel pee-pee-STREH-loh

bathing suit
il costume da bagno
eel kohs-TOO-meh dah BAH-nyoh

bathtub
la vasca da bagno
lah VAH-skah dah BAH-nyoh

beans
i fagioli
ee fah-JOH-lee

bear
l'orso (m.)
LOHR-soh

bed
il letto
eel LEH-toh

bee
l'ape (f.)
LAH-peh

beetle
lo scarabeo
loh skah-rah-BEH-oh

bell pepper
il peperone
eel peh-peh-ROH-neh

belt
la cintura
lah cheen-TOO-rah

bicycle
la bicicletta
lah bee-chee-KLEH-tah

bird
l'uccello (m.)
loo-CHEH-loh

black
nero
NEH-roh

English to Italian Word List

black currant
il ribes nero
eel REE-behs NEH-roh

blackberry
la mora
lah MOH-rah

blackboard
la lavagna
lah lah-VAH-nyah

blender
il frullatore
eel froo-lah-TOH-reh

blouse
la camicetta
lah kah-mee-CHEH-tah

blue
blu
bloo

blueberry
il mirtillo
eel meer-TEE-loh

boat
la barca
lah BAHR-kah

book
il libro
eel LEE-broh

bookcase
la libreria
lah lee-breh-REE-ah

boots
gli stivali
lee stee-VAH-lee

bow tie
il farfallino
eel fahr-fah-LEE-noh

bowl
la scodella
lah skoh-DEH-lah

bracelet
il braccialetto
eel brah-chah-LEH-toh

bread
il pane
eel PAH-neh

breakfast
la colazione
lah koh-lah-TSYOH-neh

broccoli
i broccoli
ee BROH-koh-lee

brother
il fratello
eel frah-TEH-loh

brown
marrone
mah-ROH-neh

Brussels sprouts
i cavoletti di Bruxelles
ee kah-voh-LEH-tee dee brook-SEHL

bus
l'autobus (m.)
LOW-toh-boos

butter
il burro
eel BOO-roh

butterfly
la farfalla
lah fahr-FAH-lah

cabbage
il cavolo
eel KAH-voh-loh

cafeteria
la mensa
lah MEHN-sah

cake
la torta
lah TOHR-tah

camel
il cammello
eel kah-MEH-loh

candy
le caramelle
leh kah-rah-MEH-leh

car
la macchina
lah MAH-kee-nah

cardigan
il cardigan
eel KAHR-dee-gahn

carpet
la moquette
lah moh-KEH-tuh

carrot
la carota
lah kah-ROH-tah

cashew
l'anacardo (m.)
lah-nah-KAHR-doh

cat
il gatto
eel GAH-toh

caterpillar
il bruco
eel BROO-koh

cauliflower
il cavolfiore
eel kah-vohl-FYOH-reh

celery
il sedano
eel SEH-dah-noh

cell phone
il cellulare
eel cheh-loo-LAH-reh

centipede
il millepiedi
eel mee-leh-PYEH-dee

cereal
i cereali
ee cheh-reh-AH-lee

chair
la sedia
lah SEH-dyah

cheek
la guancia
lah GWAHN-chah

cheese
il formaggio
eel fohr-MAH-joh

cherry
la ciliegia
lah chee-LYEH-jah

chestnut
la castagna
lah kahs-TAH-nyah

chin
il mento
eel MEHN-toh

chocolate
il cioccolato
eel choh-koh-LAH-toh

circle
il cerchio
eel CHEHR-kyoh

clock
l'orologio (m.)
loh-roh-LOH-joh

coat
il cappotto
eel kah-POH-toh

coconut
la noce di cocco
lah NOH-cheh dee KOH-koh

coffee
il caffè
eel kah-FEH

coffee table
il tavolino
eel tah-voh-LEE-noh

comb
il pettine
eel PEH-tee-neh

computer
il computer
eel kohm-PYOO-tehr

cookie
il biscotto
eel bee-SKOH-toh

corn
il mais
eel MAH-ees

couch
il divano
eel dee-VAH-noh

cousin (female)
la cugina
lah koo-JEE-nah

cousin (male)
il cugino
eel koo-JEE-noh

cow
la mucca
lah MOO-kah

crab
il granchio
eel GRAHN-kyoh

cranberry
il mirtillo rosso
eel meer-TEE-loh ROH-soh

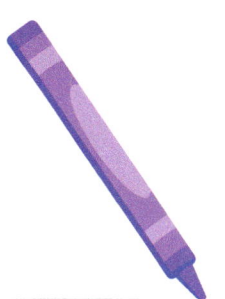

crayon
il pastello a cera
eel pahs-TEH-loh ah CHEH-rah

crocodile
il coccodrillo
eel koh-koh-DREE-loh

cucumber
il cetriolo
eel cheh-tree-OH-loh

cup
la tazza
lah TAH-tsah

curtain
la tenda
lah TEHN-dah

cycling
il ciclismo
eel chee-KLEEZ-moh

dad
il papà
eel pah-PAH

dancing
il ballo
eel BAH-loh

date
il dattero
eel DAH-teh-roh

daughter
la figlia
lah FEE-lyah

deer
il cervo
eel CHEHR-voh

desk
la scrivania
lah skree-vah-NEE-ah

dessert
il dolce
eel DOHL-cheh

diamond
il rombo
eel ROHM-boh

digger
la scavatrice
lah skah-vah-TREE-cheh

dinner
la cena
lah CHEH-nah

dishes
i piatti
ee PYAH-tee

dishwasher
la lavastoviglie
lah lah-vah-stoh-VEE-lyeh

English to Italian Word List

diving
le immersioni
leh ee-mehr-SYOH-nee

dog
il cane
eel KAH-neh

dolphin
il delfino
eel dehl-FEE-noh

door
la porta
lah POHR-tah

dress
l'abito (m.)
LAH-bee-toh

dresser
la cassettiera
lah kah-seh-TYEH-rah

dryer
l'asciugatrice (f.)
lah-shoo-gah-TREE-cheh

duck
l'anatra (f.)
LAH-nah-trah

ear
l'orecchio (m.)
loh-REH-kyoh

earrings
gli orecchini
lee oh-reh-KEE-nee

egg
l'uovo (m.)
LWOH-voh

eggplant
la melanzana
lah meh-lahn-TSAH-nah

eight
otto
OH-toh

eighteen
diciotto
dee-CHOH-toh

eighty
ottanta
oh-TAHN-tah

elbow
il gomito
eel GOH-mee-toh

elephant
l'elefante (m.)
leh-leh-FAHN-teh

elevator
l'ascensore (m.)
lah-shehn-SOH-reh

eleven
undici
OON-dee-chee

endive
l'indivia (f.)
leen-DEE-vyah

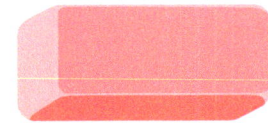

eraser
la gomma per cancellare
lah GOH-mah pehr kahn-cheh-LAH-reh

eye
l'occhio (m.)
LOH-kyoh

eyebrow
il sopracciglio
eel soh-prah-CHEE-lyoh

face
il viso
eel VEE-zoh

fan
il ventilatore
eel vehn-tee-lah-TOH-reh

faucet
il rubinetto
eel roo-bee-NEH-toh

ferry
il traghetto
eel trah-GEH-toh

fifteen
quindici
KWEEN-dee-chee

fifty
cinquanta
cheen-KWAHN-tah

fig
il fico
eel FEE-koh

finger
il dito
eel DEE-toh

fingernail
l'unghia (f.)
LOON-gyah

fire engine
il camion dei pompieri
eel KAH-myohn dey pohm-PYEH-ree

firefly
la lucciola
lah LOO-choh-lah

fish
il pesce
eel PEH-sheh

five
cinque
CHEEN-kweh

flamingo
il fenicottero
eel feh-nee-KOH-teh-roh

flip-flops
le infradito
leh een-frah-DEE-toh

floor
il pavimento
eel pah-vee-MEHN-toh

floss
il filo interdentale
eel FEE-loh een-tehr-dehn-TAH-leh

flour
la farina
lah fah-REE-nah

fly
la mosca
lah MOHS-kah

foot
il piede
eel PYEH-deh

football
il football americano
eel FOOT-bohl ah-meh-ree-KAH-noh

fork
la forchetta
lah fohr-KEH-tah

forty
quaranta
kwah-RAHN-tah

four
quattro
KWAH-troh

fourteen
quattordici
kwah-TOR-dee-chee

fox
la volpe
lah VOHL-peh

freezer
il congelatore
eel kohn-jeh-lah-TOH-reh

fries
le patate fritte
leh pah-TAH-teh FREE-teh

frog
la rana
lah RAH-nah

garbage can
la pattumiera
lah pah-too-MYEH-rah

garbage truck
il camion delle immondizie
eel KAH-myohn deh-leh ee-mohn-DEE-tsyeh

garden
il giardino
eel jahr-DEE-noh

garlic
l'aglio (m.)
LAH-lyoh

ginger
lo zenzero
loh DZEHN-dzeh-roh

giraffe
la giraffa
lah jee-RAH-fah

glass
il bicchiere
eel bee-KYEH-reh

glasses
gli occhiali da vista
lee oh-KYAH-lee dah VEE-stah

gloves
i guanti
ee GWAHN-tee

goal
la porta
lah POHR-tah

goat
la capra
lah KAH-prah

golf
il golf
eel gohlf

goose
l'oca (f.)
LOH-kah

gorilla
il gorilla
eel goh-REE-lah

granddaughter
la nipote
lah nee-POH-teh

grandfather
il nonno
eel NOH-noh

grandmother
la nonna
lah NOH-nah

grandson
il nipote
eel nee-POH-teh

grapefruit
il pompelmo
eel pohm-PEHL-moh

grapes
l'uva (f.)
LOO-vah

grasshopper
la cavalletta
lah kah-vah-LEH-tah

gray
grigio
GREE-joh

green
verde
VEHR-deh

green beans
i fagiolini
ee fah-joh-LEE-nee

guava
la guava
la GWAH-vah

gymnastics
la ginnastica artistica
lah jee-NAHS-tee-kah ahr-TEES-tee-kah

hair
i capelli
ee kah-PEH-lee

hair dryer
il fon
eel fohn

hairbrush
la spazzola
lah SPAH-tsoh-lah

hallway
l'ingresso (m.)
leen-GREH-soh

English to Italian Word List

ham
il prosciutto
eel proh-SHOO-toh

hamster
il criceto
eel kree-CHEH-toh

hand
la mano
lah MAH-noh

hat
il cappello
eel kah-PEH-loh

hazelnut
la nocciola
lah noh-CHOH-lah

head
la testa
lah TEHS-tah

heart
il cuore
eel KWOH-reh

hedgehog
il riccio
eel REE-choh

heel
il tallone
eel tah-LOH-neh

helicopter
l'elicottero (m.)
leh-lee-KOH-teh-roh

helmet
il casco
eel KAHS-koh

hen
la gallina
lah gah-LEE-nah

herbs
le erbe aromatiche
leh EHR-beh ah-roh-MAH-tee-keh

high heels
i tacchi alti
ee TAH-kee AHL-tee

hiking
le escursioni
leh ehs-koor-SYOH-nee

hippopotamus
l'ippopotamo (m.)
lee-poh-POH-tah-moh

hips
i fianchi
ee FYAHN-kee

honey
il miele
eel MYEH-leh

horse
il cavallo
eel kah-VAH-loh

horseback riding
l'equitazione (f.)
leh-kwee-tah-TSYOH-neh

hot chocolate
la cioccolata calda
lah choh-koh-LAH-tah KAHL-dah

hot-air balloon
la mongolfiera
lah mohn-gohl-FYEH-rah

ice cream
il gelato
eel jeh-LAH-toh

ice hockey
hockey su ghiaccio
OH-key soo GYAH-choh

ice skates
i pattini da ghiaccio
ee PAH-tee-nee dah GYAH-choh

ice-skating
il pattinaggio su ghiaccio
eel pah-tee-NAH-joh soo GYAH-choh

jacket
la giacca
lah JAH-kah

jam
la marmellata
lah mahr-meh-LAH-tah

jeans
i jeans
ee jeens

juice
il succo di frutta
eel SOO-koh dee FROO-tah

kale
la verza
lah VEHR-dzah

kangaroo
il canguro
eel kahn-GOO-roh

kitchen sink
il lavello
eel lah-VEH-loh

kiwi
il kiwi
eel KEE-wee

knee
il ginocchio
eel jee-NOH-kyoh

knife
il coltello
eel kohl-TEH-loh

koala
il koala
eel koh-AH-lah

ladybug
la coccinella
lah koh-chee-NEH-lah

lamp
la lampada
lah LAHM-pah-dah

leek
il porro
eel POH-roh

leg
la gamba
lah GAHM-bah

lemon
il limone
eel lee-MOH-neh

lentils
le lenticchie
leh lehn-TEE-kyeh

lettuce
la lattuga
lah lah-TOO-gah

light blue
azzurro
ah-DZOO-roh

lime
la limetta
lah lee-MEH-tah

lion
il leone
eel leh-OH-neh

lips
le labbra
leh LAH-brah

lobster
l'aragosta (f.)
lah-rah-GOH-stah

lotion
la crema per il corpo
lah KREH-mah pehr eel KOHR-poh

lunch
il pranzo
eel PRAHN-dzoh

lunch box
il portapranzo
eel pohr-tah-PRAHN-dzoh

mango
il mango
eel MAHN-goh

map
la cartina
lah kahr-TEE-nah

marker
il pennarello
eel peh-nah-REH-loh

martial arts
le arti marziali
leh AHR-tee mahr-TSYAH-lee

meat
la carne
lah KAHR-neh

melon
il melone
eel meh-LOH-neh

menu
il menù
eel meh-NOO

microwave
il microonde
eel mee-kroh-OHN-deh

milk
il latte
eel LAH-teh

mirror
lo specchio
loh SPEH-kyoh

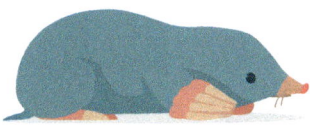

mole
la talpa
lah TAHL-pah

mom
la mamma
lah MAH-mah

monkey
la scimmia
lah SHEE-myah

mosquito
la zanzara
lah dzahn-DZAH-rah

moth
la falena
lah fah-LEH-nah

motorcycle
la motocicletta
lah moh-toh-chee-KLEH-tah

mouse
il topo
eel TOH-poh

mouth
la bocca
lah BOH-kah

mushroom
il fungo
eel FOON-goh

mustard
la senape
lah SEH-nah-peh

N

napkin
il tovagliolo
eel toh-vah-LYOH-loh

neck
il collo
eel KOH-loh

necklace
la collana
lah koh-LAH-nah

net
la rete
lah REH-teh

nine
nove
NOH-veh

nineteen
diciannove
dee-chah-NOH-veh

ninety
novanta
noh-VAHN-tah

nose
il naso
eel NAH-zoh

notebook
il quaderno
eel kwah-DEHR-noh

75

English to Italian Word List

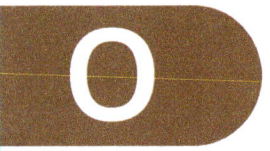

oatmeal
la farina d'avena
lah fah-REE-nah dah-VEH-nah

octopus
il polpo
eel POHL-poh

oil
l'olio (m.)
LOH-lyoh

olive
l'oliva (f.)
loh-LEE-vah

one
uno
OO-noh

one hundred
cento
CHEHN-toh

onion
la cipolla
lah chee-POH-lah

orange (color)
arancione
ah-rahn-CHOH-neh

orange (fruit)
l'arancia (f.)
lah-RAHN-chah

oval
l'ovale (m.)
loh-VAH-leh

oven
il forno
eel FOHR-noh

owl
il gufo
eel GOO-foh

painting
il quadro
eel KWAH-droh

pajamas
il pigiama
eel pee-JAH-mah

pan
la padella
lah pah-DEH-lah

panda
il panda
eel PAHN-dah

pants
i pantaloni
ee pahn-tah-LOH-nee

papaya
la papaya
lah pah-PAH-yah

parents
i genitori
ee jeh-nee-TOH-ree

parrot
il pappagallo
eel pah-pah-GAH-loh

parsnip
la pastinaca
lah pah-stee-NAH-kah

passion fruit
il frutto della passione
eel FROO-toh DEH-lah pah-SYOH-neh

pasta
la pasta
lah PAHS-tah

peach
la pesca
lah PEH-skah

peanut
l'arachide (f.)
lah-RAH-kee-deh

pear
la pera
lah PEH-rah

peas
i piselli
ee pee-ZEH-lee

pecan
la noce pecan
lah NOH-cheh peh-KAHN

pen
la penna
lah PEH-nah

pencil
la matita
lah mah-TEE-tah

penguin
il pinguino
eel peen-GWEE-noh

pepper
il pepe
eel PEH-peh

persimmon
il caco
eel KAH-koh

pie
la crostata
lah kroh-STAH-tah

pig
il maiale
eel mah-YAH-leh

pillow
il cuscino
eel koo-SHEE-noh

pineapple
l'ananas (m.)
LAH-nah-nahs

pink
rosa
ROH-zah

pistachio
il pistacchio
eel pee-STAH-kyoh

pitcher
la caraffa
lah kah-RAH-fah

plane
l'aeroplano (m.)
lie-roh-PLAH-noh

plate
il piatto
eel PYAH-toh

plum
la susina
lah soo-ZEE-nah

police car
l'auto della polizia (f.)
LOW-toh deh-lah
poh-lee-TSEE-ah

pot
la pentola
lah PEHN-toh-lah

potato
la patata
lah pah-TAH-tah

prune
la prugna secca
lah PROO-nyah SEH-kah

pumpkin
la zucca
lah DZOO-kah

purple
viola
vee-OH-lah

R

rabbit
il coniglio
eel koh-NEE-lyoh

raccoon
il procione
eel proh-CHOH-neh

radish
il ravanello
eel rah-vah-NEH-loh

rain boots
gli stivali da pioggia
lee stee-VAH-lee dah PYOH-jah

raincoat
l'impermeabile (m.)
leem-pehr-meh-AH-bee-leh

raisins
l'uvetta (f.)
loo-VEH-tah

raspberry
il lampone
eel lahm-POH-neh

rectangle
il rettangolo
eel reh-TAHN-goh-loh

red
rosso
ROH-soh

refrigerator
il frigorifero
eel free-goh-REE-feh-roh

rhinoceros
il rinoceronte
eel ree-noh-cheh-ROHN-teh

rice
il riso
eel REE-zoh

ring
l'anello (m.)
lah-NEH-loh

roof
il tetto
eel TEH-toh

room
la stanza
lah STAHN-tsah

rooster
il gallo
eel GAH-loh

rowing
il canottaggio
eel kah-noh-TAH-joh

rug
il tappeto
eel tah-PEH-toh

ruler
il righello
eel ree-GEH-loh

running
la corsa
lah KOHR-sah

S

sailboat
la barca a vela
lah BAHR-kah ah VEH-lah

sailing
la vela
lah VEH-lah

salad
l'insalata (f.)
leen-sah-LAH-tah

salami
il salame
eel sah-LAH-meh

salt
il sale
eel SAH-leh

sandals
i sandali
ee SAHN-dah-lee

sandwich
il panino
eel pah-NEE-noh

sausage
la salsiccia
lah sahl-SEE-chah

scarf
la sciarpa
lah SHAHR-pah

scissors
le forbici
leh FOHR-bee-chee

scooter
il monopattino
eel moh-noh-PAH-tee-noh

English to Italian Word List

sea star
la stella marina
lah STEH-lah mah-REE-nah

seahorse
il cavalluccio marino
eel kah-vah-LOO-choh mah-REE-noh

seal
la foca
lah FOH-kah

seven
sette
SEH-teh

seventeen
diciassette
dee-chah-SEH-teh

seventy
settanta
seh-TAHN-tah

shallot
lo scalogno
loh skah-LOH-nyoh

shampoo
lo shampoo
loh SHAHM-poh

shark
lo squalo
loh SKWAH-loh

sheep
la pecora
lah PEH-koh-rah

shelf
lo scaffale
loh skah-FAH-leh

ship
la nave
lah NAH-veh

shirt
la camicia
lah kah-MEE-chah

shorts
i pantaloncini corti
ee pahn-tah-lohn-CHEE-nee KOHR-tee

shoulders
le spalle
leh SPAH-leh

shower
la doccia
lah DOH-chah

sink
il lavandino
eel lah-vahn-DEE-noh

sister
la sorella
lah soh-REH-lah

six
sei
sey

sixteen
sedici
SEH-dee-chee

sixty
sessanta
seh-SAHN-tah

skateboarding
andare con lo skateboard
ahn-DAH-reh kohn loh SKEYT-bohrd

skiing
lo sci
loh shee

skirt
la gonna
lah GOH-nah

skunk
la puzzola
lah POO-tsoh-lah

slippers
le pantofole
leh pahn-TOH-foh-leh

snake
il serpente
eel sehr-PEHN-teh

sneakers
le scarpe da ginnastica
leh SKAHR-peh dah jee-NAHS-tee-kah

soap
il sapone
eel sah-POH-neh

soccer
il calcio
eel KAHL-choh

socks
i calzini
ee kahl-TSEE-nee

soda
la bibita
lah BEE-bee-tah

son
il figlio
eel FEE-lyoh

soup
la zuppa
lah TSOO-pah

soybeans
i germogli di soia
ee jehr-MOH-lee dee SOH-yah

sparkling water
l'acqua frizzante (f.)
LAH-kwah free-DZAHN-teh

spices
le spezie
leh SPEH-tsyeh

spider
il ragno
eel RAH-nyoh

spinach
gli spinaci
lee spee-NAH-chee

spoon
il cucchiaio
eel koo-KYAH-yoh

square
il quadrato
eel kwah-DRAH-toh

squirrel
lo scoiattolo
loh skoh-YAH-toh-loh

stadium
lo stadio
loh STAH-dyoh

stairs
le scale
leh SKAH-leh

star
la stella
lah STEH-lah

stove
il fornello
eel fohr-NEH-loh

strawberry
la fragola
lah FRAH-goh-lah

subway
la metropolitana
lah meh-troh-poh-lee-TAH-nah

sugar
lo zucchero
loh TSOO-keh-roh

suit
il completo
eel kohm-PLEH-toh

sunglasses
gli occhiali da sole
lee oh-KYAH-lee dah SOH-leh

surfing
fare surf
FAH-reh surf

sweater
il maglione
eel mah-LYOH-neh

sweet potato
la patata dolce
lah pah-TAH-tah DOHL-cheh

swimming
il nuoto
eel NWOH-toh

T-shirt
la maglietta
lah mah-LYEH-tah

table
il tavolo
eel TAH-voh-loh

table tennis
il tennis da tavolo
eel TEH-nees dah TAH-voh-loh

tablecloth
la tovaglia
lah toh-VAH-lyah

taxi
il taxi
eel TAHK-see

tea
il tè
eel teh

tea kettle
la teiera
lah teh-YEH-rah

teeth
i denti
ee DEHN-tee

television
la televisione
lah teh-leh-vee-ZYOH-neh

ten
dieci
DYEH-chee

tennis
il tennis
eel TEH-nees

tennis racket
la racchetta da tennis
lah rah-KEH-tah dah TEH-nees

thirteen
tredici
TREH-dee-chee

thirty
trenta
TREHN-tah

three
tre
treh

tie
la cravatta
lah krah-VAH-tah

tiger
la tigre
lah TEE-greh

tights
i collant
ee koh-LAHN

toaster
il tostapane
eel tohs-tah-PAH-neh

toenail
l'unghia
LOON-gyah

toes
le dita dei piedi
leh DEE-tah dey PYEH-dee

toilet
la toilette
lah twah-LEH-tuh

toilet paper
la carta igienica
lah KAHR-tah ee-JEH-nee-kah

tomato
il pomodoro
eel poh-moh-DOH-roh

toothbrush
lo spazzolino
loh spah-tsoh-LEE-noh

toothpaste
il dentifricio
eel dehn-tee-FREE-choh

towel
l'asciugamano (m.)
lah-shoo-gah-MAH-noh

toys
i giocattoli
ee joh-KAH-toh-lee

English to Italian Word List

train
il treno
eel TREH-noh

triangle
il triangolo
eel tree-AHN-goh-loh

truck
il camion
eel KAH-myohn

tummy
la pancia
lah PAHN-chah

tuna
il tonno
eel TOH-noh

turkey
il tacchino
eel tah-KEE-noh

turtle
la tartaruga
lah tahr-tah-ROO-gah

twelve
dodici
DOH-dee-chee

twenty
venti
VEHN-tee

two
due
DOO-eh

U

uncle
lo zio
loh TSEE-oh

underwear
l'abbigliamento intimo (m.)
lah-bee-lyah-MEHN-toh EEN-tee-moh

uniform
l'uniforme (f.)
loo-nee-FOHR-meh

V

van
il furgoncino
eel foor-gohn-CHEE-noh

vase
il vaso
eel VAH-zoh

vest
il gilet
eel jee-LEH

vinegar
l'aceto (m.)
lah-CHEH-toh

volleyball
la pallavolo
lah pah-lah-VOH-loh

W

waffles
le cialde
leh CHAHL-deh

walnut
la noce
lah NOH-cheh

washer
la lavatrice
lah lah-vah-TREE-cheh

water
l'acqua (f.)
LAH-kwah

watermelon
l'anguria (f.)
lahn-GOO-ryah

whale
la balena
lah bah-LEH-nah

wheat
il grano
eel GRAH-noh

whipped cream
la panna montata
lah PAH-nah mohn-TAH-tah

white
bianco
BYAHN-koh

whiteboard
la lavagna magnetica
lah lah-VAH-nyah mah-NYEH-tee-kah

window
la finestra
lah fee-NEHS-trah

wolf
il lupo
eel LOO-poh

worm
il verme
eel VEHR-meh

wrestling
la lotta
lah LOH-tah

wrist
il polso
eel POHL-soh

Y

yellow
giallo
JAH-loh

yogurt
lo yogurt
loh YOH-goort

Z

zebra
la zebra
lah DZEH-brah

zero
zero
DZEH-roh

zucchini
la zucchina
lah dzoo-KEE-nah